Extinct exhibitionist.

Weirdosaurus.

Prehistory's most peculiar creatures

for the weirdos :)

© 2025 Quarto Publishing Group USA Inc.
Text and illustration: © 2025 Philip Bunting

Philip Bunting has asserted his right to be identified
as the author and illustrator of this work.

Designers: Philip Bunting & Sarah Chapman-Suire
Senior Commissioning Editor: Carly Madden
Editor: Nancy Dickmann
Consultant: Dr Nick Crumpton
Creative Director: Malena Stojić
Associate Publisher: Rhiannon Findlay
Senior Production Controller: Elizabeth Reardon

First published in 2025 by Happy Yak, an imprint of The Quarto Group.
100 Cummings Center, Suite 265D
Beverly, MA 01915, USA.
T (978) 282-9590 F (978) 283-2742
EEA Representation, WTS Tax d.o.o., Žanova ulica 3, 4000 Kranj, Slovenia
www.quarto.com

No part of this publication may be reproduced, stored in a retrieval
system, or transmitted in any form, or by any means, electrical,
mechanical, photocopying, recording or otherwise, without
the prior written permission of the publisher or a licence
permitting restricted copying.

All rights reserved.

ISBN 978 0 7112 9582 7

Manufactured in Guangdong, China TT062025
9 8 7 6 5 4 3 2 1

Contents.

32 Silesaurus.
32 Teraterpeton.
33 Drepanosaur.
34 Triopticus primus.
35 Sharovipteryx.
35 Eudimorphodon.
36 Caelestiventus.
36 Terrestrisuchus.
37 Daemonosaurus chauliodus.

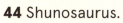

4 Introduction.
10 A word on terrible lizards.
11 How to use this book.

12 Triassic Period.
14 Eotitanosuchus.
15 Lystrosaurus.
15 Thrinaxodon.
16 Eretmorhipis.
17 Mastondonsaurus.
17 Hupehsuchus.
18 Erythrosuchus.
18 Shringasaurus.
19 Atopodentatus.
20 Arizonasaurus.
22 Tanystropheus.
23 Thalattosaurus.
24 Scleromochlus.
24 Hyperodapedon.
26 Hypuronector.
28 Longisquama.
29 Placerias.
29 Metoposaurus.
30 Stagonolepis.
30 Carnufex.
31 Henodus.

38 Jurassic Period.
40 Lesothosaurus.
40 Scelidosaurus.
41 Pegomastax.
42 Cryolophosaurus.
43 Lufengosaurus.
43 Dilophosaurus.
44 Kulindadromeus.
44 Shunosaurus.
45 Huayangosaurus.
46 Tianchisaurus.
47 Proceratosaurus.
48 Anchiornis.
48 Epidexipteryx.
49 Jeholopterus.
50 Dicraeosaurus.
52 Guanlong.
53 Mamenchisaurus.
53 Rhamphorhynchus.
54 Ambopteryx.
54 Yingshanosaurus.
55 Brachiosaurus.
56 Gargoyleosaurus.
56 Hesperosaurus.
57 Chilesaurus.
58 Chaoyangsaurus.
58 Fruitadens.
59 Archaeopteryx.

60 Cretaceous Period.
62 Bajadasaurus.
63 Concavenator.
64 Amargasaurus.
66 Microraptor.
66 Nigersaurus.
67 Incisivosaurus.
68 Caudipteryx.
69 Pterodaustro.
69 Suzhousaurus.
70 Psittacosaurus.
71 Oryctodromeus.
72 Spinosaurus.

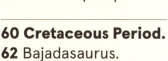

74 Parasaurolophus.
75 Nyctosaurus.
76 Gigantoraptor.
77 Einiosaurus.
78 Carnotaurus.
79 Kosmoceratops.
80 Euoplocephalus.
81 Tsintaosaurus.
82 Lambeosaurus.
84 Rhinorex.

85 Halszkaraptor.
85 Chirostenotes.
86 Masiakasaurus.
87 Qianzhousaurus.
87 Therizinosaurus.
88 Pachycephalosaurus.
90 Quetzalcoatlus.
91 Mononykus.
91 Nedoceratops.

92 The end?
96 Index.

Introduction.

About sixty-six million years have passed since the age of the dinosaurs ended. Pretty much everything we know about these wonderful weirdies comes from a relatively small number of fossilized bones, feathers, and skins. Those few rocky remains are the only real proof we have that dinosaurs and other ancient animals once prowled, pranced, and plodded upon the planet we call home.

Fossilized bones can provide a general idea of what these amazing animals might have looked like. We can estimate their size and approximate shape, how they may have moved, and even what they ate for breakfast. However, after so many millions of years in the ground, very few clues remain to indicate how the softer stuff on the outside might have looked. Muscles, skin, feathers, quills, frills, and even beaks most often get lost in the rock (just as an elephant's trunk, a kangaroo's pouch, or my big ears would not survive fossilization).

Every dinosaur drawing, movie, or model you've ever seen is simply the result of some hairy human's best possible guess. We're making a lot of it up, based on a few clues from the fossil record (and in some cases the features of a few of their existing descendants). Although we now know a lot about dinosaurs, we still can't be 100 percent certain what the owner of that skeleton *really* looked like, all those millions of years ago.

It might have looked like this . . .

Dinosaurus traditionalus.
(Terrible lizard in the familiar form)

Or this...
Dinosaurus ornis.
(Terrible lizard in the feathered form)

Or even this!
Dinosaurus ridiculous.
(Now that's just ridiculous. Really...)

Oy!

For now, paleontologists (scientists who study fossilized life), illustrators, and dabblers (like you and me) gather clues and use clever science techniques to figure out what bygone beasties might have really looked like. But more and more fossils are unearthed every year, and our technology is always improving. So perhaps one day you might find a way to figure out how those old weirdies *really* looked!

A word on terrible lizards.

The word "dinosaur" is an odd one. It was coined in the 1800s by an English biologist named Sir Richard Owen. "Dinosaur" is based on two Greek words: *deinos* (meaning "terrible") and *sauros* (meaning "lizard"). I'll leave you to judge whether they were terrible or not, but it's a fact that no dinosaurs were actually lizards. All dinosaurs were reptiles, sure, but lizards occupy their own scaly branch of the tree of life.

In the spirit of Sir Richie's fast-and-loose naming conventions, this book contains more than just true dinosaurs. While *Weirdosaurus* contains *mostly* dinosaurs, it also presents a good smattering of flying reptiles (not dinosaurs), swimming reptiles (not dinosaurs), amphibians (not dinosaurs), lizards (not dinosaurs), archosaurs (not all dinosaurs) . . . . All right, you get the picture.

How to use this book.

Weirdosaurus is a collection of the most peculiar creatures from the time we know as the Mesozoic Era (252–66 million years ago). The Mesozoic was made up of three periods: the Triassic, the Jurassic, and the Cretaceous. Every creature featured presents the same set of stats and specifics:

Navigational arrow. Points from the text to its illustration

Illustration. Lots of guesswork here, as discussed

Name translation. The actual meaning of the animal's name

Animal name. Generally a scientific name, which tends to be made up of old Greek words

When it lived. MYA stands for "million years ago"

Size comparison. Its size compared to a modern animal (or thing)

Diet. Very generally:
Carnivore: Meat
Herbivore: Plants
Insectivore: Insects
Omnivore: Mixed
Piscivore: Fish

Length. Head to tail, unless noted

▲ **Archaeopteryx.**
(Ancient wing)

- 149–145 MYA
- Carnivore
- 20 in. (50 cm)

When the first Archaeopteryx fossil was discovered, people were very confused. Birds were not known to have lived so long ago. Some people even thought it was evidence of an angel. With its broad, feathered wings, talons, and small body (about the size of a crow), it definitely has a lot in common with modern birds, but it also had sharp teeth and a long, bony tail.

Description. Brief background information about the weirdie

Triassic Period.
252–201 million years ago.

Dinosaurs first emerged in the mid-Triassic, among a great variety of truly remarkable reptiles, absurd amphibians, and more. The Triassic began following a humongous extinction event—known as the Permian-Triassic Extinction—when volcanic eruptions are thought to have caused the Earth's climate to warm rapidly, wiping out around 90 percent of all species at the time. Yeesh!

Eotitanosuchus.
EE-oh-tie-TAN-oh-SOO-kus
page 14

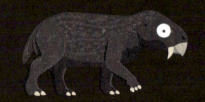

Lystrosaurus.
LISS-tro-SAWE-us
page 15

Thrinaxodon.
Thrih-NAK-soh-DON
page 15

Eretmorhipis.
Eh-ret-mor-HI-pis
page 16

Mastodonsaurus.
MAS-toh-don-SAWR-us
page 17

Hupehsuchus.
HOO-pay-SOO-kus
page 17

Erythrosuchus.
Eh-RITH-roh-SUU-kus
page 18

Shringasaurus.
SHRING-guh-SAWR-us
page 18

Atopodentatus.
AH-toh-po-den-TAH-tus
page 19

Arizonasaurus.
Ar-ih-ZOH-nah-SAWR-us
page 20

Tanystropheus.
TAN-ee-STROH-fee-us
page 22

Thalattosaurus.
Thuh-LAT-oh-SAWR-us
page 23

Scleromochlus.
🔊 SKLER-oh-MOK-Lus
page 24

Hyperodapedon.
🔊 HIGH-per-oh-DA-peh-don
page 24

Hypuronector.
🔊 High-PYOO-roh-NEK-tor
page 26

Longisquama.
🔊 LONG-iss-KWAH-ma
page 28

Placerias.
🔊 Pla-SEER-ee-as
page 29

Metoposaurus.
🔊 Meh-TOH-poh-SAWR-us
page 29

Stagonolepis.
🔊 Sta-GON-oh-lep-iss
page 30

Carnufex.
🔊 CAR-noo-fex
page 30

Henodus.
🔊 HEN-oh-dus
page 31

Silesaurus.
🔊 SIGH-lee-SAWR-us
page 32

Teraterpeton.
🔊 TAIR-ah-TER-peh-ton
page 32

Drepanosaur.
🔊 Dreh-PAN-oh-saur
page 33

Triopticus primus.
🔊 Try-OP-ti-kus PRI-mus
page 34

Sharovipteryx.
🔊 SHA-roh-VIP-teh-riks
page 35

Eudimorphodon.
🔊 YOO-die-MOR-foh-don
page 35

Caelestiventus.
🔊 Say-LES-ti-VEN-tus
page 36

Terrestrisuchus.
🔊 Teh-RES-tri-SOO-kus
page 36

Daemonosaurus.
🔊 DAY-moh-nuh-SAWR-us
page 37

Eotitanosuchus.
(Dawn titan crocodile)

- 267 MYA
- Carnivore
- 20 ft. (6 m)

Cock-a-doodle don't!

Never smile at a dawn titan crocodile.

Fangs for the ~~memories~~ → nightmares!

Sit! Roll over! Heel! Looking a little bit like the most terrifying terrier you've ever seen in your life, Eotitanosuchus belonged to a group more closely related to mammals than other reptiles (and they were certainly not crocs, despite the name). However, at around the size of a whole pack of dogs, this is clearly not one puppy you'd want to play fetch with.

Lystrosaurus really dug Triassic life.

Could burrow underground, like a hairless, toothy badger!

▲ Lystrosaurus.
(Shovel lizard)

- 250 MYA
- Herbivore
- 3–8 ft. (1–2.5 m)

▼ Thrinaxodon.
(Trident tooth)

- 250–245 MYA
- Carnivore
- 20 in. (50 cm)

With a parrot-ish beak, short, walrus-y tusks, a wombat-like body, stumpy legs, and a Labrador's tail, Lystrosaurus looked like a mashed-up drawing of a made-up monster. Looks aside, this bizarre beastie was one of prehistory's greatest survivors, making it through a pre-Triassic extinction event that wiped out around 90 percent of all species at the time.

Sporting whiskers, fur, and a distinctive dog-like face (just without the pointy ears), Thrinaxodon was one of a group of reptile-like mammal ancestors called cynodonts. Perhaps it would have made a better playmate for a game of fetch?

Mesozoic mullet.

Warning: Do not call Thrinaxodon "Whiskers."

May have had a moist nose—a bit like a cat!

Triassic Period | 15

Small, bony plates ran down its back like an aquatic Stegosaur!

Mother Nature went quackers.

Oarsome flippers.

Eretmorhipis.
(Oar fan)

- 250 MYA
- Piscivore
- 28 in. (70 cm)

When Western scientists first came across the modern-day platypus, they assumed these odd creatures were a hoax, thanks to their incredible combination of features. Yet a similar grab bag of a creature existed millions of years ago! So it's not hard to see why this odd aquatic animal has been dubbed the "platypus of the Triassic" thanks to its broad bill, streamlined body, and paddle-shaped flippers.

16 | Triassic Period

Mastodonsaurus was the largest amphibian ever!

Tusk, tusk! →

◀ Mastodonsaurus.
(Teat tooth lizard)

- 247–201 MYA
- Omnivore
- 20 ft. (6 m)

At a glance, this alarmingly enormous amphibian ancestor looked quite a lot like a smooth, chubby crocodile, but Mastodonsaurus was actually a distant ancestor of frogs! This very big, very scary frog-to-be packed two large tusks in its lower jaw, which poked up through two conveniently placed holes in its face. These would have been a wonderful way for Mastodonsaurus to hold on to its slippery supper.

Messed-up maritime mishmash!

Terror of Triassic tiddlers.

▶ Hupehsuchus.
(Hupeh crocodile)

- 247–237 MYA
- Piscivore
- 3 ft. (1 m)

What would you get if you crossed an iguana, a pelican, and a whale? This little monster would have to come pretty close! Despite its dolphin-ish appearance, this species was puny in comparison, at only 3 feet (1 meter) long. With tiny, sharp teeth and a throat that ballooned out as it swam along, Hupehsuchus would gulp up huge mouthfuls of water and fish, and then strain out its lunch through filtering structures in its jaws.

Red Crocs: first in fashion 247 million years ago.

Don't sit behind it at the movies.

▲ Erythrosuchus.
(Red crocodile)

- 247–200 MYA
- Carnivore
- 16 ft. (5 m)

The largest land predator of its day was known for having a *really* big head. No, they weren't really into themselves—they literally had a gigantic noggin. In fact, Erythrosuchus's head was so big it took up almost a third of its body length! In human terms, that would be like our head stretching down to the bottom of our rib cage. Weird.

Females may have had small **horns** or no horns at all.

▶ Shringasaurus.
(Horned lizard)

- 247 MYA
- Herbivore
- 10–13 ft (3–4 m)

Bulky and stout with a long, thick neck, the males of this species of lumbering land lizard were bestowed with a large pair of bull-like horns. These were likely used to attract females and to fight off rivals. Or perhaps it's just a clever ploy to pull the focus away from their comically tiny heads?

Atopodentatus is the oldest-known seafaring vegetarian!

▶ Atopodentatus.
(Unusually toothed)

- 244 MYA
- Herbivore
- 8–10 ft. (2.5–3 m)

So this is where the design of the vacuum nozzle came from! Atopodentatus's head might look like a cross between a vacuum and a hammerhead shark, but this ocean-loving weirdo put its flattened face to good use, nipping algae off rocks and then sucking in water through its needle-like teeth. The teeth acted as a filter, just like a whale's baleen.

I tried to slip a VACUUM joke in here, but they all SUCK.

A tail (nearly) as old as time.

Triassic Period | 19

Life in the Triassic was far from plain sailing.

Arizonasaurus.
(Lizard from Arizona)

- 243 MYA
- Carnivore
- 10 ft. (3 m)

This desert-dweller boasted long, bony spines on its back, which are thought to have supported an impressive sail-like structure. The sail wasn't used for swimming (or sailing) though, but rather it is believed it may have been used for thermoregulation, helping the creature keep cool on those hot desert days. The sail may have also doubled as a calling card to attract a mate, to help them keep warm on those cold desert nights.

Tanystropheus.
(Long-necked one)

- 242 MYA
- Piscivore
- 16 ft. (5 m)

Imagine if an evil genius spliced a giraffe and a Komodo dragon . . . . Ta-da! This guy. This oddly proportioned Triassic terror had a neck three times the length of its body. Tanystropheus put that neck to good use, often sneaking up on its prey in murky water, striking when they least expected it. Go, go gadget neck! Research suggests that Tanystropheus spent most of the time in the water, but it may also have ambushed its prey from the water's edge, a bit like a modern-day heron.

The joke about this neck is too long → to tell.

Scientists recently unearthed a partially fossilized Tanystropheus fart.* They described it as "a blast from the past." ↓

*Very serious disclaimer: This is just a joke.

22 | **Triassic Period**

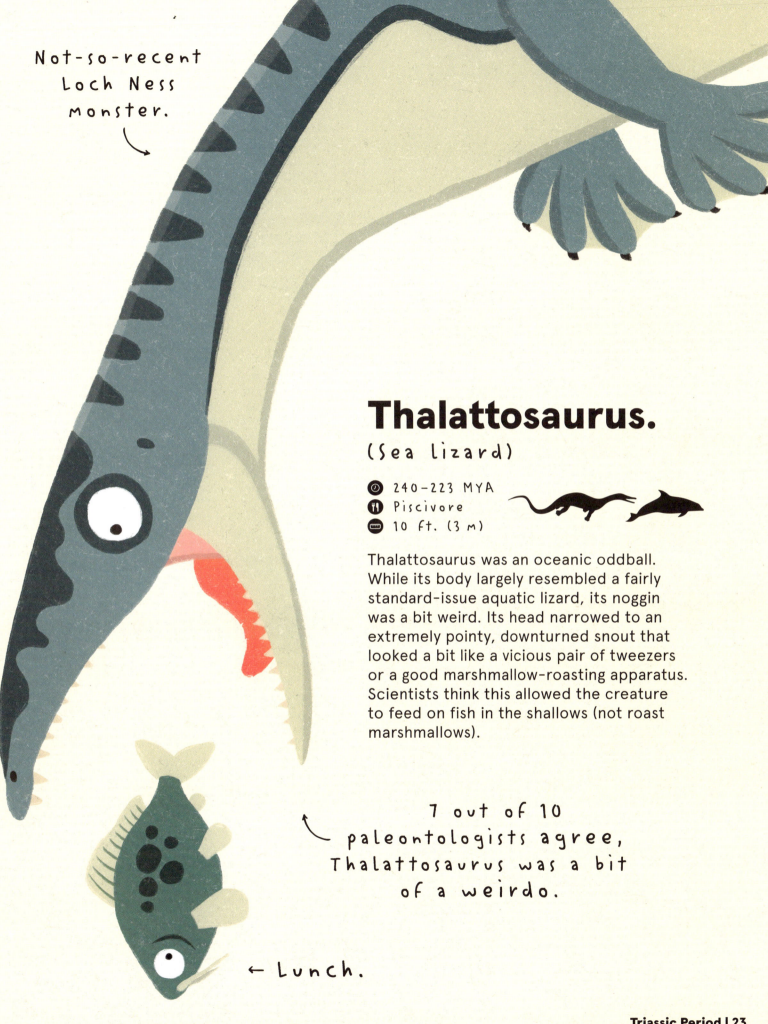

Not-so-recent Loch Ness monster.

Thalattosaurus.
(Sea lizard)

- 240–223 MYA
- Piscivore
- 10 ft. (3 m)

Thalattosaurus was an oceanic oddball. While its body largely resembled a fairly standard-issue aquatic lizard, its noggin was a bit weird. Its head narrowed to an extremely pointy, downturned snout that looked a bit like a vicious pair of tweezers or a good marshmallow-roasting apparatus. Scientists think this allowed the creature to feed on fish in the shallows (not roast marshmallows).

7 out of 10 paleontologists agree, Thalattosaurus was a bit of a weirdo.

← Lunch.

▼ Scleromochlus.
(Hard lever)

- 240–201 MYA
- Insectivore
- 8 in. (20 cm)

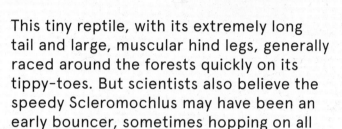

This tiny reptile, with its extremely long tail and large, muscular hind legs, generally raced around the forests quickly on its tippy-toes. But scientists also believe the speedy Scleromochlus may have been an early bouncer, sometimes hopping on all fours in a similar way to a rabbit.

Dino-soar!

Dino-land.

May have been an early ancestor of flying pterosaurs.

← Scleromochlus always had a spring in its step.

▶ Hyperodapedon.
(Excessively toothed)

- 237–200 MYA
- Herbivore
- 7 ft. (2 m)

This curious creature managed to combine the protruding incisor teeth of a naked mole rat with the beak-like mouth of a snapping turtle. Yikes! But what Hyperodapedon lacked in looks, it made up for in its ability to Win At Life. It was a born survivor, with fossils proving that it lived on every continent except Australia and Antarctica, in vast numbers, for millions of years.

Hypuronector.
(Deep-tailed swimmer)

- 237–201 MYA
- Insectivore
- 5 in. (12 cm)

Once thought to be aquatic, due to its oversized, paddle-like tail, it is now widely accepted that this dainty and unusual chameleon-like creature actually lived its life in the trees. Some paleontologists even think Hypuronector may have had patagia (skin flaps between its legs), to help it glide from branch to branch, like a flying squirrel.

↑ Unbeleafable camouflage.

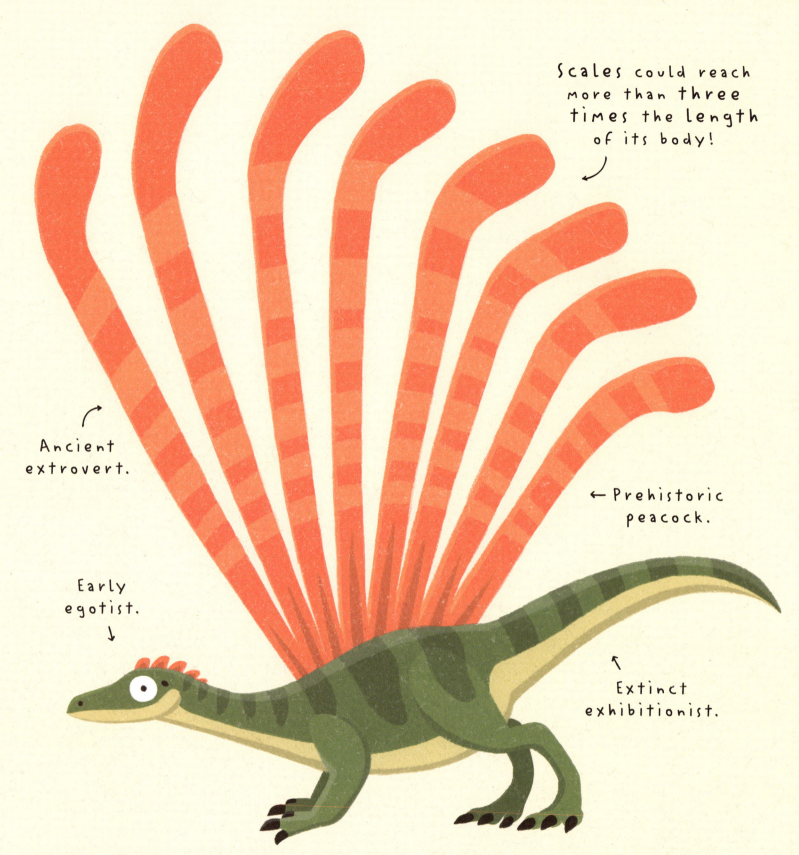

Scales could reach more than three times the length of its body!

Ancient extrovert.

← Prehistoric peacock.

Early egotist.

↗ Extinct exhibitionist.

Longisquama.
(Long scales)

- 240–220 MYA
- Insectivore
- 4 in. (9 cm)

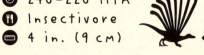

One of prehistory's greatest show-offs, this tiny tree-dwelling reptile used those oversized scales to send a message. Similar to peacocks, lyrebirds, and frilled-neck lizards, their appendages may have been used to impress a mate or scare off predators. Or perhaps these tiny creatures just made really good hockey stick holders.

▶ Placerias.
(Broad body)

- 237–208 MYA
- Herbivore
- 7–12 ft. (2–3.5 m)

This barrel-shaped beastie weighed as much as a grand piano and was the biggest herbivore of its time. Its odd appearance made it look a little bit like a young rhino dressed up as Dracula for Halloween, with its stout body and huge, fang-like tusks pointing downward from its beak-like mouth. We could end on a vampire pun here, but they tend to suck.

Placerias: a sight for saur eyes.

Upside-downo rhino.

Supersized salamander.

▲ Metoposaurus.
(Front lizard)

- 237–201 MYA
- Piscivore
- 10 ft. (3 m)

With its broad, flattened head, tiny eyes, thick, swishy tail, and rather unfortunately short, weak limbs, this portly, piscivorous prowler was like the super-salamander of the Triassic waterways. Scientists think it would hide itself on the bottom of a riverbed and suck unsuspecting prey into its huge, chompy jaws. Definitely a game of hide-and-seek you don't want to play.

▼ Stagonolepis.
(Drop-shaped scale)

- 237 MYA
- Herbivore
- 3 m

Very **vegan** croc. Awww!

This scaly scrapper lurks on one of the older branches of the crocodilian family tree—a distant ancestor of modern-day crocs and alligators. But this is one croc you could have cuddled up to (unless you happened to be a Triassic turnip). Unlike the rest of its fearsome family, Stagonolepis was actually a herbivore. Its flat teeth were used for chewing plants and ferns and the pointed tip at the front of its jaw was used for digging up plant roots.

▶ Carnufex.
(Butcher)

- 237–228 MYA
- Carnivore
- 10 ft. (3 m)

Very **fast** croc. Argh!

Crocodiles are totally terrifying in the water, but if you've ever seen one lumbering awkwardly on land, you realize you could quite easily outrun it. Not so with the "Butcher of Carolina," another ancient croc ancestor who could sprint toward you on its two long, muscly legs! Well, I know what I'm having nightmares about tonight.

I'm suddenly feeling blue.

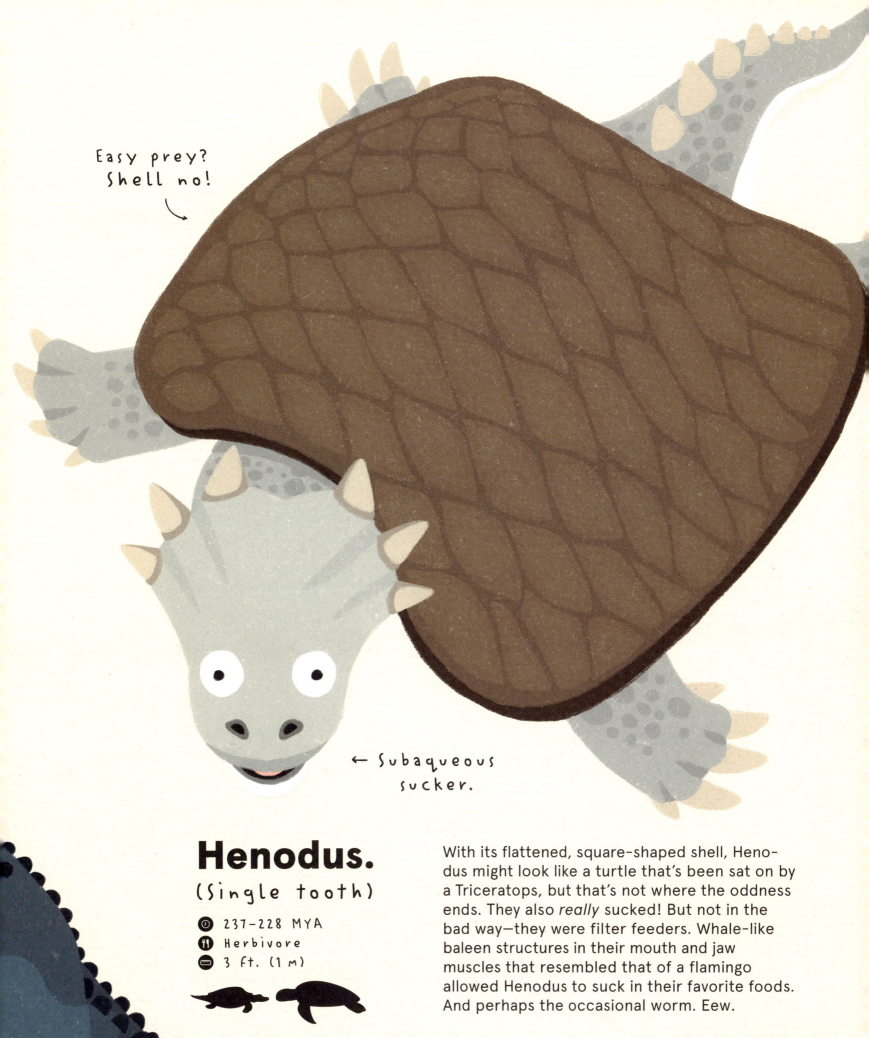

Easy prey? Shell no!

← Subaqueous sucker.

Henodus.
(Single tooth)

- 237–228 MYA
- Herbivore
- 3 ft. (1 m)

With its flattened, square-shaped shell, Henodus might look like a turtle that's been sat on by a Triceratops, but that's not where the oddness ends. They also *really* sucked! But not in the bad way—they were filter feeders. Whale-like baleen structures in their mouth and jaw muscles that resembled that of a flamingo allowed Henodus to suck in their favorite foods. And perhaps the occasional worm. Eew.

Triassic Period | 31

← Do you think he saurus?

↱ Impeckable posture.

← Silesaurus likely pecked at the ground for food, like a chicken!

▲ Silesaurus.
(Silesian lizard)

- 237–208 MYA
- Herbivore
- 8 ft. (2.3 m)

The clues left by its fossils suggest that this beak-faced beastie should have roamed around upright on two legs, yet its oddly long and slender front legs suggest that Silesaurus actually pecked about on all fours.

▼ Terraterpeton.
(Wonderful creeping thing)

- 237–228 MYA
- Herbivore
- 3 ft. (1 m)

Is it a bird? A lizard? A crocodile? Evolution went to town on Teraterpeton! With its long, mostly toothless pelican-like beak and sturdy reptilian body, "confused creepy thing" might have been a more apt name?

↑ Teraterpeton: wonderfully creepy.

32 | Triassic Period

Drepanosaur.
(Sickle lizard)

- 235–201 MYA
- Insectivore
- 12–24 in. (30–60 cm)

Sometimes referred to as a monkey lizard thanks to its prehensile tail, Drepanosaur was a small, agile tree-dweller. It looked a little like someone stuck a tiny, bird-like head on to a chameleon's body, and then—just to crank up the weirdness, they gave it some long, sloth-like claws . . . and one more at the end of its tail for good measure! That's one monkey we could do without meeting on our next tree climb.

Always trying to get over the hump.

Yikes!

Drepanosaur used its long claws to open up bark to find grubs and beetles.

← Bonus tail claw!

Triassic Period | 33

Triopticus primus was one of the first reptiles to sport a dome-shaped skull. Long before its Cretaceous cousins (see page 88).

Dome → divot.

The tail flap is thought to have helped Eudimorphodon steer during flight.

▲ Triopticus primus.
(The first of three eyes)

- 228–220 MYA
- Unknown
- Unknown

This reptile sounds a bit like a robo-villain, but translate it and you realize the name describes this creature's oddest feature. It got this cool name because on the top of its dome-shaped skull was something resembling a third eye. Disappointingly, it was actually just an indented pit in the skull that seems to have served no function.

▼ Sharovipteryx.
(Sharov's wonderful wing)

- 225 MYA
- Omnivore
- 10 in. (25 cm)

Leaping lizards! This one-of-a-kind tree-dwelling reptile is the first and only known creature to have a gliding membrane attached to its incredibly long hind legs and tail, rather than to its arms. This gave it the ability to glide effortlessly from tree to tree using a triangular-shaped gliding surface, a bit like a rather terrifying, tiny hang-glider.

This ~~weird~~ "unique" leg-wing design has **never** appeared in nature again! ↓

↑ Sharov's wonderful grin.

Pterrifying pteeth! ↓

◀ Eudimorphodon.
(True dimorphic tooth)

- 215 MYA
- Piscivore
- 3 ft. (1 m)

This toothsome pterosaur was a dentist's dream (and a fish's nightmare), with 110 teeth tightly packed into its tiny 3-inch (7-centimeter) snout. Most pterosaurs had teeth that were all of a similar size and shape, and some had no teeth at all. But Eudimorphodon scored big in the tooth department, with a chilling range of treacherous choppers, including large fangs and pointy, serrated teeth. Perfect for munching all kinds of sea life, from bony fish to hard-shelled invertebrates.

Triassic Period | 35

Caelestiventus is thought to be the largest Triassic pterosaur.

Frightful flapper.

▲ Caelestiventus.
(Divine wind)

- 208 MYA
- Carnivore
- 5 ft. wingspan

This freaky flyer was not named after its heavenly farts. And in fact, there's not much that's "divine" about this terrifying pterosaur with its gigantic, lumpy head, jowly chin, razor-sharp teeth, long, whip-like tail, and huge wingspan. Perhaps "the Devil's wind" would have been more apt?

▼ Terrestrisuchus.
(Land crocodile)

- 208–201 MYA
- Carnivore
- 3 ft. (1 m)

Terrestrisuchus looked like a greyhound-sized crocodile on a crash diet. But what really set this odd croc apart from the snappy pack were its long and slender legs. Most members of the crocodilian family have legs splayed out to the sides of their body, but this croc's legs supported its body from underneath.

Leggy land lover.

← Terrestrisuchus's long legs indicate that it was built for speed.

36 | Triassic Period

Pre-dated toothpaste by 208–201 million years.

"Evil spirit lizard" comes from the place its fossil was found: Ghost Ranch, New Mexico, USA.

Daemonosaurus chauliodus.

(Buck-toothed evil spirit lizard)

- 208–201 MYA
- Carnivore
- 5 ft. (1.5 m)

At first glance, you might almost think this delicate-looking reptile is cute, with its large eyes and short, blunt snout. But the minute it opened its mouth and gave you its characteristic smile, you'd see this buck-toothed beastie certainly lived up to its name. Not only were its teeth slanted forward at the front, they also had the largest tooth-to-skull-size ratio of any predatory dinosaur. Keep those fingers close, kiddies!

Triassic Period | 37

Jurassic Period.
201–145 million years ago.

Dinosaurs ruled the Earth during the Jurassic Period. Over many millions of years, humongous plant-eaters emerged alongside predatory meat-munching dinos, lizards, and birds. The Jurassic played host to an incredible diversity of weird and wonderful animal species, which thrived in a warm, humid climate.

Lesothosaurus.
🔊 Leh-SOH-toe-SAWR-us
page 40

Scelidosaurus.
🔊 Ske-LIGH-doh-SAWR-us
page 40

Pegomastax.
🔊 Peg-oh-MASS-taks
page 41

Cryolophosaurus.
🔊 Kry-oh-LOH-foh-SAWR-us
page 42

Lufengosaurus.
🔊 Loo-FENG-oh-SAWR-us
page 43

Dilophosaurus.
🔊 Dye-LOH-foh-SAWR-us
page 43

Kulindadromeus.
🔊 Koo-LIN-dah-DROH-me-us
page 44

Shunosaurus.
🔊 SHOO-no-SAWR-us
page 44

Huayangosaurus.
🔊 Hwah-YANG-oh-SAWR-us
page 45

Tianchisaurus.
🔊 TYAN-chee-SAWR-us
page 46

Proceratosaurus.
🔊 PROH-se-RA-toh-SAWR-us
page 47

Anchiornis.
🔊 AN-kee-OR-nis
page 48

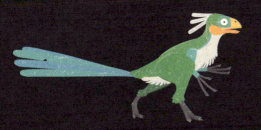
Epidexipteryx.
🔊 EP-ih-dek-SIP-ter-IKS
page 48

Jeholopterus.
🔊 YEH-hol-OP-ter-us
page 49

Dicraeosaurus.
🔊 Dye-KRAY-oh-SAWR-us
page 50

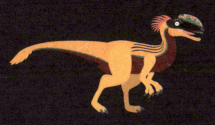
Guanlong.
🔊 Gwan-long
page 52

Mamenchisaurus.
🔊 Mah-MEN-chee-SAWR-us
page 53

Ramphorhynchus.
🔊 RAM-foh-RING-kus
page 53

Ambopteryx.
🔊 Am-BOP-teh-riks
page 54

Yingshanosaurus.
🔊 YING-SHAN-oh-SAWR-us
page 54

Brachiosaurus.
🔊 BRAK-ee-oh-SAWR-us
page 55

Gargoyleosaurus.
🔊 GAR-GOY-loh-SAWR-us
page 56

Hesperosaurus.
🔊 HES-per-oh-SAWR-us
page 56

Chilesaurus.
🔊 CHEE-leh-SAWR-us
page 57

Chaoyangsaurus.
🔊 CHOW-YANG-SAWR-us
page 58

Fruitadens.
🔊 FROO-ta-dens
page 58

Archaeopteryx.
🔊 AR-kee-OP-ter-iks
page 59

Two-legged trendsetter.

Lesothosaurus was an upstanding citizen of the Jurassic.

▲ Lesothosaurus.
(Lesotho lizard)

- 201–176 MYA
- Herbivore
- 3 ft. (1 m)

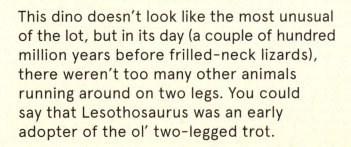

This dino doesn't look like the most unusual of the lot, but in its day (a couple of hundred million years before frilled-neck lizards), there weren't too many other animals running around on two legs. You could say that Lesothosaurus was an early adopter of the ol' two-legged trot.

▼ Scelidosaurus.
(Limb lizard)

- 208–194 MYA
- Herbivore
- 13 ft. (4 m)

This herbivore's skin was entirely covered in an array of bony spikes and plates to protect it from its many toothsome predators. It also had rather fetching and fierce-looking horns at the back of its relatively tiny head. Scelidosaurus was an early ancestor of both the stegosaurs and the ankylosaurs.

The world's first complete dinosaur skeleton belonged to a Scelidosaurus.

Saur ankles.

Pegomastax.
(Strong jaw)

- 201–190 MYA
- Herbivore
- 24 in. (60 cm)

You certainly wouldn't want to bump into this weird turkey-hedgehog-vampire-chicken in the middle of the night. Even when you know it only eats plants, Pegomastax is still terrifying! No one is sure why it was covered in spiky quills, but most believe it was either for defense or for impressing potential mates.

We don't know why this vegetarian had such large, sharp canines in its beak. Were prehistoric plants more vicious, perhaps? →

↑ When you stand on a Lego brick.

↑ Why did the Pegomastax cross the road?*

*Because the chicken wasn't around yet.

Dinky Diplodocus.

Its strong hind legs allowed Lufengosaurus to reach high into trees.

◀ Lufengosaurus.
(Lufeng lizard)

- 195–190 MYA
- Herbivore
- 20 ft (6 m)

You do not want to declare a thumb war with this guy. It was an early relative of the more massive sauropods—a group of long-necked, long-tailed (generally very long!) plant-eaters. This reptile could not only walk on four legs or two, it also sported five digits on each of its front limbs, with a rather enormous and sharp claw on each "thumb." This deadly thumb was likely used for defense, given its strictly vegan diet.

▶ Dilophosaurus.
(Two-crested lizard)

- 190 MYA
- Carnivore
- 20 ft. (6 m)

It might look like it has a taco strapped to its head, but believe it or not, this dino was the most feared and fearsome predator of its time. The spec-taco-lar crest was believed to be brightly colored and designed to attract the interest of the opposite sex. Some scientists even think the crest may have been topped with inflatable air sacs for extra "look at me" factor, like some modern birds have on their throats.

Tacosaurus.

No frills.

Jurassic Period | 43

▶ Kulindadromeus.
(Kulinda runner)

- 174–145 MYA
- Herbivore
- 3 ft. (1 m)

Scientists once thought that feathers were unique to theropods (the group that includes T. rex and other forebears of modern birds). But this two-legged, plant-eating weirdie belonged to the ornithopods—a group of beaked, plant-eating dinos such as Parasaurolophus (see page 74). Its fossils show simple, hair-like feathers, along with more complex ones. This discovery provided evidence that feathers were common among many different types of dinosaurs.

Feather-brain.

▲ Shunosaurus.
(Lizard from Sichuan)

- 170–160 MYA
- Herbivore
- 33 ft. (10 m)

Shunosaurus might have been smaller than some of its more giant cousins (such as Brachiosaurus on page 55 or Mamenchisaurus on page 53), but it had a secret weapon those other big guys didn't have. This shrunken sauropod packed a terrifyingly heavy, spiky club at the end of its tail, capable of seeing off an attacker in one swift blow.

▼ Huayangosaurus.
(Lizard from Huayang)

- 170–163 MYA
- Herbivore
- 13 ft. (4 m)

This early stegosaur is a prickly little character. Not content with the double row of long spikes stretching from its neck to the tip of its tail, it also managed to sprout two extra spikes, sticking out sideways, just above its forelimbs. At a prehistoric party, Huayangosaurus was not an animal you'd want to rub shoulders with.

Smallest-known stegosaur. Aww!

↑ A spiky character.

Huayangosaurus: a shoulder to cry ~~on~~ about.

You don't want to be a part of this club. ↓

↑ Some paleontologists say they were noisy sleepers, and so should be renamed "Shunosnoreus."

Tianchisaurus.
(Heavenly pool lizard)

- 170–166 MYA
- Herbivore
- 13 ft. (4 m)

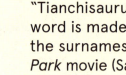

This little battler might just win the competition for having the most peculiar name (and not just the heavenly pool bit). Its species name is "Tianchisaurus nedegoapeferima." The second word is made up from the first two letters of the surnames of the cast of the original *Jurassic Park* movie (Sam **Ne**ill, Laura **De**rn, Jeff **Go**ldblum, Richard **At**tenborough, Bob **Pe**ck, Martin **Fe**rrero, Ariana **Ri**chards, and Joseph **Ma**zzello).
Looks like they forgot to include the "t" from Attenborough? Paleontologists: weirdos.

Armored eyebrows!

Bulletproof beak.

Hard-as toenails.

46 | Jurassic Period

Its prey may have sneezed to death.

↑ Sharp, serrated teeth, like steak knives. Ouchy!

See this fluff? You're going down.

Proceratosaurus.
(Lizard before Ceratosaurus)

- 167–164 MYA
- Carnivore
- 10 ft. (3 m)

This teensy yet toothsome tyrant is actually the oldest-known relative of the rather more enormous T. rex. While the unusual crest on its snout may have been for display, another theory is that it might have helped reduce the pressure on the skull while the dino was munching its prey.

Jurassic Period | 47

▼ Anchiornis.
(Near bird)

- 167–150 MYA
- Insectivore
- 13 in. (34 cm)

This chicken-sized dino was covered in feathers from head to toe. However, those feathers were a bit useless, as they were too short to help it fly any great distance. Instead, Anchiornis would have glided from branch to branch. This was the first dinosaur fossil to provide evidence of the animal's original color. By analyzing fossilized feather cells, scientists have been able to predict the hue of Anchiornis's plumage, with 90 percent certainty. It is thought to have been black and white with a reddish crest, similar to a woodpecker.

Woody Woodpecker's great, great, great gazillion granny.

Anchiornis's feathers were no good for flying but acted like an excellent parachute.

Jurassic jodhpurs.

▶ Epidexipteryx.
(Display feather)

- 164–161 MYA
- Insectivore
- 10 in. (24 cm)

This odd-looking hodgepodge would be absolutely terrifying were it not so tiny! In fact, Epidexipteryx was one of the smallest non-avian dinosaurs to ever exist (avian dinosaurs were—and indeed still are—birds). Those four long tail feathers are thought to have been purely for the purpose of showing off to potential mates.

48 | Jurassic Period

▶ Jeholopterus.
(Jehol wing)

- 164–161 MYA
- Insectivore
- 35 in. (90 cm) wingspan

To the insects of the mid-Jurassic, this little pterosaur was a real-life bat out of hell. An IRL Draculasaurus! Jeholopterus were toothy, bitey pterosaurs who liked nothing better than to feast on nice big, juicy Jurassic bugs. Gross!

↑ Argh!

↙ Tiny T. rex at the carnival.

↑ Flagrantly fancy feathers.

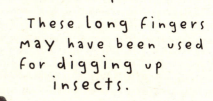

↖ These long fingers may have been used for digging up insects.

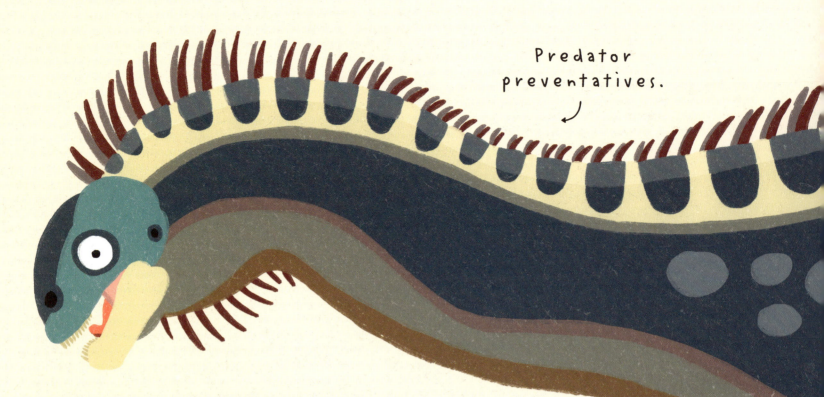

Predator preventatives.

Too big to fail!

Dicraeosaurus.
(Forked lizard)

- 163–145 MYA
- Herbivore
- 39 ft. (12 m)

This dino was a sauropod, but while its closest cousins had long necks and tiny heads, Dicraeosaurus stands apart thanks to its comparatively large noggin and short, wide neck. Its name comes from the double row of spines that extend from its head and down along its backbone. These spines may have helped put off any meat lovers who might try to eat it. "This dinner is too spiky, Mama!"

Jurassic Period | 51

These jokes are starting to dragon.

The kind of chameleon bad karma brings.

Ridiculous russet ruff.

Guanlong.
(Crowned dragon)

- 163–158 MYA
- Carnivore
- 7 ft. (2.5 m)

This "crowned dragon" had a rather show-stopping decoration on its face. Its crest was only about as thick as a tortilla, so it would have been incredibly delicate. Some paleontologists think the crest was brightly colored, and possibly even able to change color! Truth be told, it's a little hard to look terrifying when you have a colorful Mexican snack strapped to your nose.

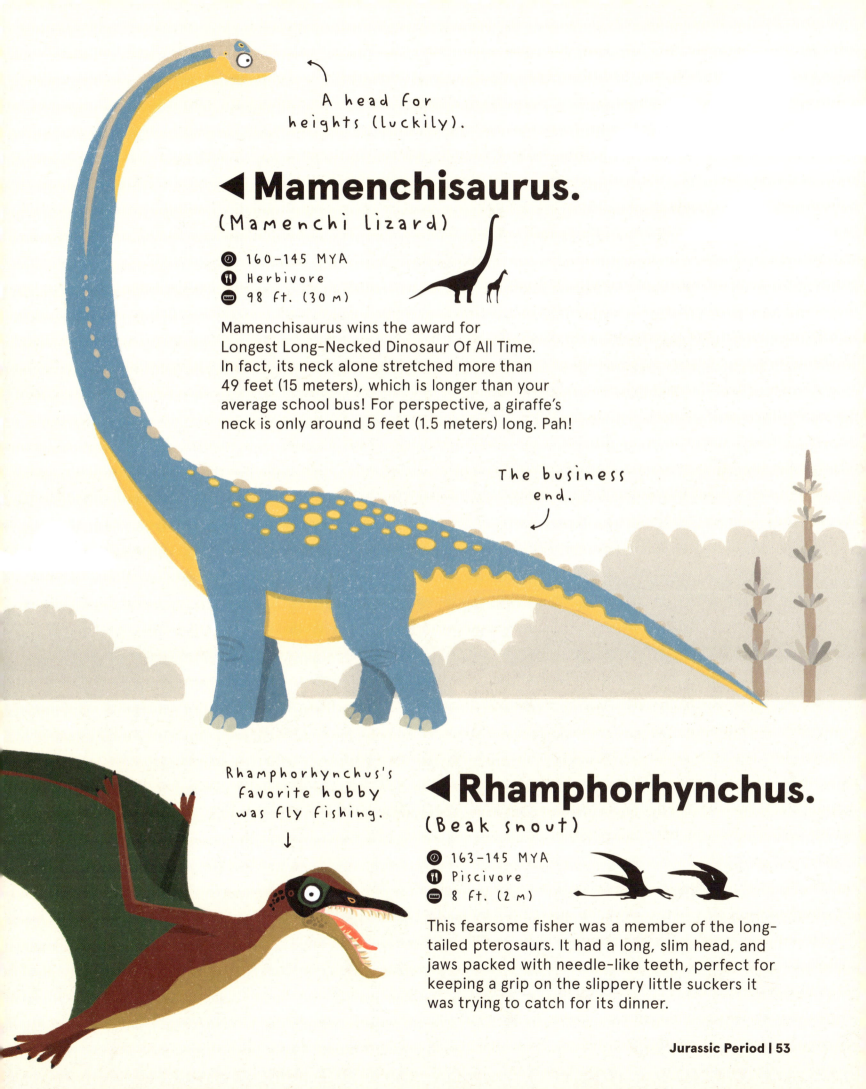

A head for heights (luckily).

◀ Mamenchisaurus.
(Mamenchi lizard)

- 160–145 MYA
- Herbivore
- 98 ft. (30 m)

Mamenchisaurus wins the award for Longest Long-Necked Dinosaur Of All Time. In fact, its neck alone stretched more than 49 feet (15 meters), which is longer than your average school bus! For perspective, a giraffe's neck is only around 5 feet (1.5 meters) long. Pah!

The business end.

Rhamphorhynchus's favorite hobby was fly fishing.

◀ Rhamphorhynchus.
(Beak snout)

- 163–145 MYA
- Piscivore
- 8 ft. (2 m)

This fearsome fisher was a member of the long-tailed pterosaurs. It had a long, slim head, and jaws packed with needle-like teeth, perfect for keeping a grip on the slippery little suckers it was trying to catch for its dinner.

▲ Ambopteryx.
(Both wings)

- 160 MYA
- Omnivore
- 12 in. (30 cm)

The forests of Jurassic China were home to one highly unusual tree dweller. If you saw a small, fluffy shape scurrying along the branches, you might have mistaken it for an early squirrel, but when it spread its long, leathery wings, it suddenly transformed into something more like a long-legged bat with tail feathers. Shudder.

▼ Yingshanosaurus.
(Mt. Ying Lizard)

- 159–142 MYA
- Herbivore
- 13–16 ft. (4–5 m)

This plant muncher had all the usual stegosaur family features: spine plates, tail spikes, tiny brain . . . (yawn!). But what set it apart from its spiky cousins were the two large, wing-like spines, about 31 inches long, that extended from its shoulders, making it look like it stole the wings off the Greek God Hermes's sandals.

Lord of the wings.

Standard stegosaur spikes.

Jurassic toot.

Very serious disclaimer: Like modern birds, Ambopteryx probably could not fart.

Forehead nostrils? Super-long neck? Could be evolutionary adaptations to avoid its very smelly feet. Pee-ew!

◀ Brachiosaurus.
(Arm lizard)

- 154–150 MYA
- Herbivore
- 79 ft. (24 m)

Unlike most other sauropods, Brachiosaurus's front legs were longer than its back legs, giving it an upright appearance. But the nostrils that sat on top of its head were an even weirder feature. Scientists once thought these may have acted as a snorkel if it went for a deep dip, but they now think the air from the nasal passages helped prevent Brachiosaurus's brain from overheating. Eating an ice cream quickly also could have helped!

▼ Gargoyleosaurus.
(Gargoyle lizard)

- 154–142 MYA
- Herbivore
- 13 ft. (4 m)

This small, armored ankylosaur certainly looked like it wasn't to be messed with. It had sharp bumps all over its back, and also sported a series of sharp spikes running along each side of its body. Clearly, this was a dinosaur that enjoyed its personal space.

▶ Hesperosaurus.
(Western lizard)

- 154–-142 MYA
- Herbivore
- 20 ft. (6 m)

With its delightful plates and deadly thagomizer (those four spikes on its tail), Hesperosaurus stomped around this planet millions of years before its famous cousin, Stegosaurus. It is also one of the few dinosaurs to have left fossilized impressions of its skin. Its lower half was covered with small, hexagonal scales while higher up, the larger scales formed rosette-like shapes. Fancy!

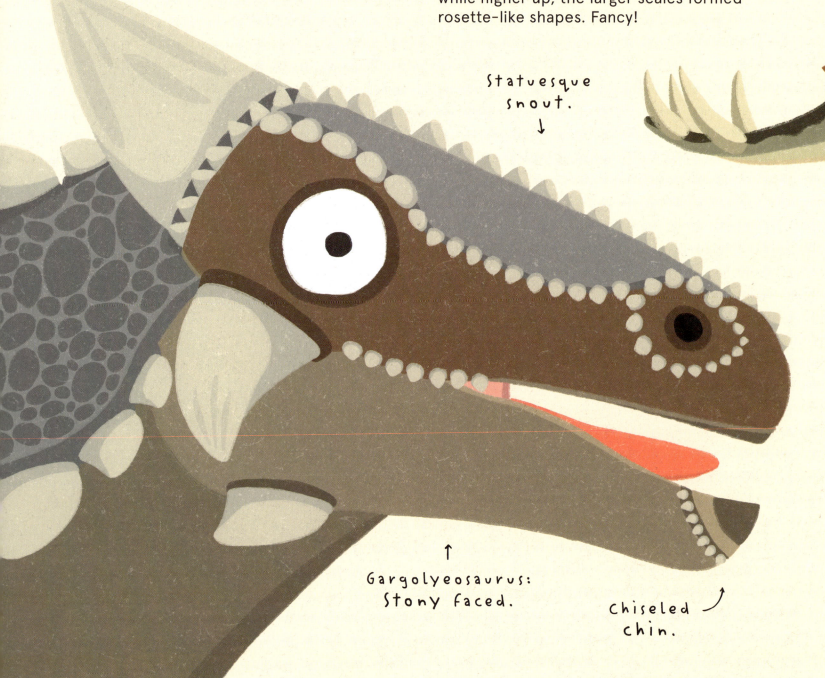

Statuesque snout. ↓

↑ Gargolyeosaurus: Stony faced.

Chiseled chin. ↗

Some say Hesperosaurus's plates helped it regulate its body temperature.*

*Others say they were just for showing off.

V. rex (vegetarian T. rex).

▶ **Chilesaurus.**
(Lizard from Chile)

- 152–145 MYA
- Herbivore
- 7–10 ft. (2–3 m)

You know when you find it hard to believe you're related to someone because you look *so* different? Chilesaurus had two fingers on each hand, just like T. rex, but that's where the resemblance ends. This creature was vegetarian, with a small head, long neck, slender body, and rather chunky arms. Paleontologists are still trying to figure out exactly where it fits on the dinosaur family tree!

Jurassic Period | 57

▶ Chaoyangsaurus.
(Chaoyang lizard)

- 152–145 MYA
- Herbivore
- 3 ft. (1 m)

Chaoyangsaurus is the earliest-known ceratopsian. This dino family is characterizedby a bony frill on the back of the skull, a beaked mouth, and a herbivorous diet (see Einiosaurus page 77, Kosmoceratops page 79, and Nedoceratops page 91). Chaoyangsaurus is thought to have had porcupine-like quills on its lower back and tail too (ouch!).

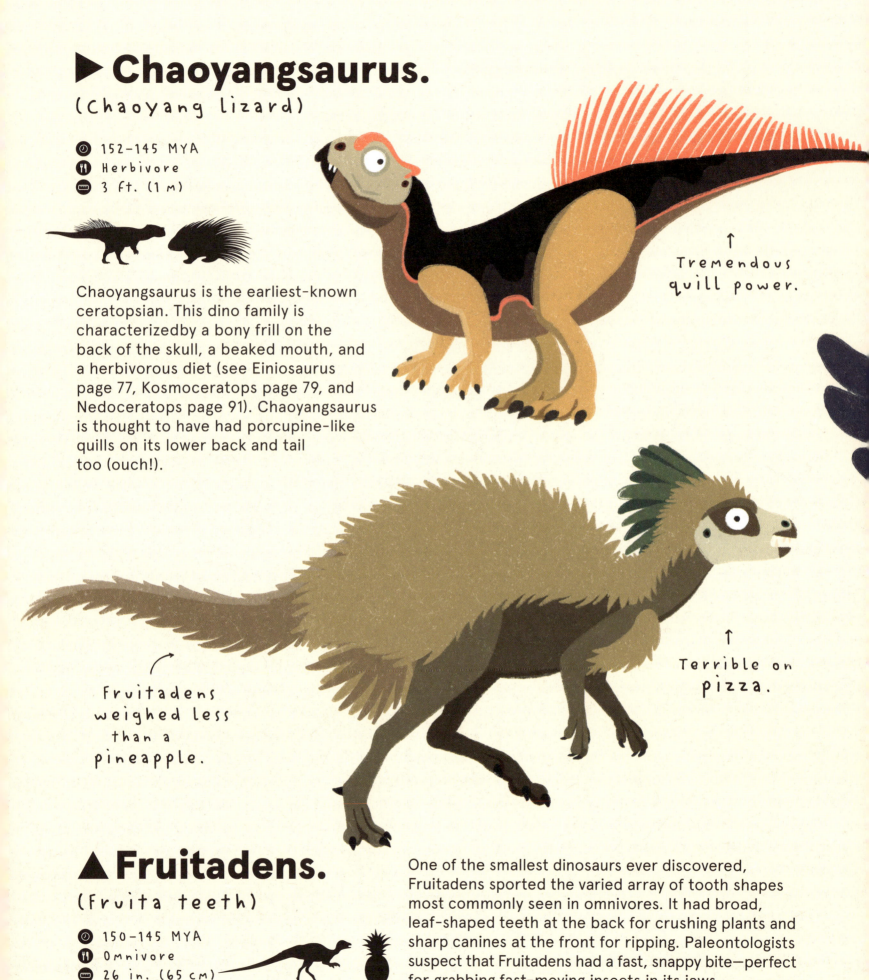

↑ Tremendous quill power.

↷ Fruitadens weighed less than a pineapple.

↑ Terrible on pizza.

▲ Fruitadens.
(Fruita teeth)

- 150–145 MYA
- Omnivore
- 26 in. (65 cm)

One of the smallest dinosaurs ever discovered, Fruitadens sported the varied array of tooth shapes most commonly seen in omnivores. It had broad, leaf-shaped teeth at the back for crushing plants and sharp canines at the front for ripping. Paleontologists suspect that Fruitadens had a fast, snappy bite—perfect for grabbing fast-moving insects in its jaws.

▼ Archaeopteryx.
(Ancient wing)

- 149–145 MYA
- Carnivore
- 20 in. (50 cm)

When the first Archaeopteryx fossil was discovered, people were very confused. Birds were not known to have lived so long ago. Some people even thought it was evidence of an angel. With its broad, feathered wings, talons, and small body (about the size of a crow), it definitely had a lot in common with modern birds, but it also had sharp teeth and a long, bony tail.

Early bird.

Jurassic squawk!

Archaeopteryx was no angel.

Jurassic Period | 59

Cretaceous Period.
145–66 million years ago.

The Cretaceous was the third and final great age of the dinosaurs. This era gave rise to some super-famous 'sauruses such as Tyrannosaurus, Velociraptor, and Triceratops—as well as this gaggle of weirdies—before ending with a bit of a bang (see page 92).

Bajadasaurus.
Bah-HAH-dah-SAWR-us
page 62

Concavenator.
KON-kah-ven-AH-tor
page 63

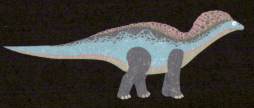

Amargasaurus.
Ah-MAR-gah-SAWR-us
page 64

Microraptor.
MY-kro-RAP-tor
page 66

Nigersaurus.
NEE-zhair-SAWR-us
page 66

Incisivosaurus.
In-SIGH-zee-voh-SAWR-us
page 67

Caudipteryx.
Kaw-DIP-ter-IKS
page 68

Pterodaustro.
TAIR-oh-DOW-stroh
page 69

Suzhousaurus.
SOO-zhoh-SAWR-us
page 69

Psittacosaurus.
Sit-TAK-oh-SAWR-us
page 70

Oryctodromeus.
Or-IK-toh-DROH-me-us
page 71

Spinosaurus.
SPY-no-SAWR-us
page 72

Parasaurolophus.
PAIR-uh-saw-RAH-Luh-fus
page 74

Nyctosaurus.
🔊 NIK-toh-SAWR-us
page 75

Gigantoraptor.
🔊 Jai-GAN-toh-RAP-tor
page 76

Einiosaurus.
🔊 EYE-nee-oh-SAWR-us
page 77

Carnotaurus.
🔊 CAR-no-TAW-rus
page 78

Kosmoceratops.
🔊 KOZ-moh-SAIR-ah-tops
page 79

Euoplocephalus.
🔊 YOO-op-loh-SEF-uh-lus
page 80

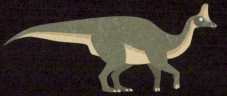
Tsintaosaurus.
🔊 SIN-TOW-sawr-us
page 81

Lambeosaurus.
🔊 LAM-bee-oh-SAWR-us
page 82

Rhinorex.
🔊 RYI-no-rex
page 84

Halszkaraptor.
🔊 HALSH-kah-RAP-tor
page 85

Chirostenotes.
🔊 Ky-ROH-sten-OH-teez
page 85

Masiakasaurus.
🔊 MAH-zhee-AH-kah-SAUR-us
page 86

Qianzhousaurus.
🔊 CHIEN-jow-SAWR-us
page 87

Therizinosaurus.
🔊 THAIR-ih-ZIN-oh-SAWR-us
page 87

Pachycephalosaurus.
🔊 PAK-ee-SEF-uh-loh-SAWR-us
page 88

Quetzalcoatlus.
🔊 KET-zal-koh-AHT-lus
page 90

Mononykus.
🔊 MON-oh-NYE-kus
page 91

Nedoceratops.
🔊 NED-oh-SAIR-ah-tops
page 91

Cretaceous Period | 61

Prehistoric punk.

Life was all downhill for Bajadasaurus.

Bajadasaurus.
(Downhill lizard)

- 140 MYA
- Herbivore
- 39 ft. (12 m)

Bajadasaurus had huge spines running down the length of its neck, but uniquely among sauropods, they faced forward. This massive, bony mohawk was likely used as a form of defense, protecting its head and neck from hungry predators. Or perhaps it was for moshing out to prehistoric punk anthems.

Concavenator.
(Hump-backed hunter)

- 130–125 MYA
- Carnivore
- 13 ft. (4 m)

Concavenator's lumpy hump was weird enough, but this dinosaur had a second strange feature: "quill knobs" sprouting from its arms. Knobs like these are generally only seen on the wing bones of modern birds. Scientists think that this otherwise scaly theropod may have sprouted fancy, colorful feathers during mating season. Forget roses, this dino busts out elbow feathers to impress its date!

Cretaceous Casanova.

Dressed to impress.

Ancient A-C.

Amargasaurus.
(Bitter Lizard)

- 129–122 MYA
- Herbivore
- 30–33 ft. (9–10 m)

Speaking of weird hairdos, the parallel double row of spines down this dinosaur's back make it look like it's sporting the world's best prehistoric mullet. Scientists aren't quite sure what those spines were for. Some think they could have been used to deter predators, while others surmise that they were covered by skin, creating a sail-like structure to help this gentle giant stay cool.

Cretaceous Period | 65

One of the smallest dinosaurs in the fossil record.

The tooth fairy's Cretaceous cash cow.

▲ Microraptor.
(Small thief)

- 125–113 MYA
- Carnivore
- 30 in. (77 cm)

This teensy dino packs a lot of weird into one very small package. Despite boasting four wings (one on each limb) rather than a paltry two, scientists aren't sure if Microraptor was actually capable of flight, or if it was more of an early glider, like modern flying squirrels.

◀ Nigersaurus.
(Niger lizard)

- 125–100 MYA
- Herbivore
- 30 ft. (9 m)

Nigersaurus was a tooth fairy's dream, with around 500 teeth, all positioned at the front of its mouth. These gnashers were ideal for grazing on low-lying vegetation. Each tooth had nine replacement teeth behind it, ready to take over when one eventually wore down or broke. Cha-ching!

The prehistoric prototype for Bugs Bunny. ↓

Gnaww, cute!

▶ Incisivosaurus.
(Incisor lizard)

- 125–122 MYA
- Herbivore
- 3 ft. (1 m)

This buck-toothed beauty has been perplexing paleontologists for years. Not only do those beaver-like front teeth look odd, they *are* odd for a theropod. Incisivosaurus might be related to meat-eating dinos like T. rex, but its rat-like buckteeth (suitable for gnawing) and jaws filled with flat teeth (suited to grinding) suggest this dinosaur was a vegetarian. Sometimes referred to as the "bunnysaurus" because . . . well, I'm sure you can figure it out!

Cretaceous Period | 67

Caudipteryx.
(Tail feather)

- 125 MYA
- Omnivore
- 35 in. (90 cm)

Its chicken feet, feathered body, and bird-like beak aren't the most unusual characteristics of Caudipteryx. Look a little further and at the end of its tail you'll see its most bizarre asset: its fan-shaped tail resembles a small peacock's display. And that's precisely what it was for—communication and attracting the opposite sex. Let's just say, it knew how to shake a tail feather.

Cocky crest.

Preposterous plumage!

What should you do if you find a blue Caudipteryx? Try to cheer it up!

Poserosaurus.

68 | Cretaceous Period

Pterodaustro: not-so-pretty in pink.

◀ Pterodaustro.
(South wing)

- 125–100 MYA
- Piscavore
- 10 ft. (3m) wingspan

This pelican-like pterosaur had 500 pairs of elastic, bristle-like structures lining its lower jaw, similar to a whale's baleen. This has led scientists to believe it was probably a filter feeder, scooping up water and straining it for tiny animals such as shrimp and other small crustaceans.

Its crazy-long claws were likely used for reaching and pulling down branches and high foliage.

Edward Scissorhands + dodo = this weirdie.

▶ Suzhousaurus.
(Suzhou lizard)

- 115 MYA
- Herbivore
- 20 ft. (6m)

The mishmash of features that was Suzhousaurus would have weighed in at around 2,900 pounds—as much as a small car. Those rather terrifying 3-feet-long claws may have been used to help harvest its leafy lunch, while deterring carnivorous onlookers.

Psittacosaurus.
(Parrot lizard)

- 100 MYA
- Herbivore
- 7 ft. (2 m)

Some scientists think that this parrot-faced, porcupine-tailed peculiarity could have been the world's first nut-eating dinosaur. It is thought that it used its beak-like jaw in a similar way to a modern parrot, cracking open hard nuts and chewing seeds. Fossils show they also ate stones to help them digest their fibrous dinners.

Who's a pretty boy then?

Psittacosauruses started life on all fours, but could stand by around age 6.

Psittacosaurus: a bit nutty.

70 | Cretaceous Period

Oryctodromeus.
(Digging runner)

- 100–93 MYA
- Herbivore
- 7 ft. (2 m)

Oryctodromeus was the first-known burrowing dinosaur. Its fossils were discovered in a den, complete with an S-bend that made it harder for predators to enter. This dino's broad snout and wide hips helped it keep stable while it dug. It is thought the burrows may have helped it survive fierce climates . . . and even fiercer predators.

Burrowing dinosaurs have been discovered in Australia, South Africa, and Korea.

Dinosnore.

Big head! Almost 6 feet (2 meters) long.

This should make you sit up straight!

Longer than three African elephants!

What could be scarier than a Spinosaurus? Two Spinosauruses!

Spinosaurus.
(Spined lizard)

- 99–93 MYA
- Carnivore/Piscivore
- 59 ft. (18 m)

On a scale of one to T. rex, this colossal carnivore was off the charts. Spinosaurus was the longest carnivorous dinosaur of them all (yep, even longer than T. rex). Fossils show its diet consisted mainly of fish, and that it would have been a comfortable swimmer, suggesting it spent most of its time in the water. Spinosaurus had a row of huge spines down its back, which were believed to support an impressive sail-like structure. Paleontologists think the sail was used for display purposes and to help this dino keep its cool in the hot Cretaceous sun.

Mesozoic megaphone.

Not a snorkel.

Parasaurolophus mooved in herds, a bit like cows.

Parasaurolophus.
(Near crested lizard)

- 98–65 MYA
- Herbivore
- 33 ft. (10 m)

If you think poor old Parasaurolophus looks like it has a trumpet strapped to the back of its head, you're not too far off the mark. That long, bony structure actually had acoustic properties that likely allowed this plant-loving dino to communicate with other members of its herd, across vast distances.

Nyctosaurus.
(Night lizard)

- 89–66 MYA
- Piscivore
- 7 ft. (2 m) wingspan

Flying reptiles are weird enough, right? But then this thing comes along with a quite frankly extravagant, antler-like protrusion sticking out of its noggin. What was it for? Extending the wi-fi? Drying its undies? No one really knows. Some scientists think it was just for impressing a mate, while others have theorized that it may have had another membrane stretching right over the top, like a huge head sail!

Nyctosaurus excelled at the first bit of the YMCA dance.

Pterosaurs went to the bathroom very quietly. (Silent P . . .)

The only pterosaur to lose the three little fingers on its wing.

Cretaceous Period | 75

Gigantoraptor.
(Giant thief)

- 83–70 MYA
- Omnivore
- 26 ft. (8 m)

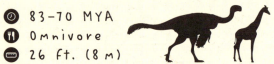

This weirdie may have had a toothless beak and a relatively squat, turkey-like head that made it look comically cartoonish, but don't be fooled—it was no cuddly character! As tall as a giraffe, with powerful legs and large clawed hands, Gigantoraptor would've been a match for any Cretaceous carnivore.

Good luck trying to make drumsticks out of this towering turkey!

76 | Cretaceous Period

The original blue rinse.

Beak careful! Gigantoraptor was as tall as a double-decker bus.

Einiosauruses lived in herds, similar to modern bison.

Einiosaurus.
(Bison lizard)

- 83–72 MYA
- Herbivore
- 13 ft. (4 m)

Einiosaurus certainly had some fabulous frill action going on, but what really set it apart was the gigantic, forward-curving horn, just above the snout. Some paleontologists suggest the shape of the horn indicates that this fancy face furniture was used primarily for display, rather than defense.

Carnotaurus.
(Meat-eating bull)

- 83–66 MYA
- Carnivore
- 26 ft. (8 m)

Those conical horns are what gives this unusual dino the "bull" part of its name. And scientists think that Carnotaurus may have even used its horns for head-to-head combat, a bit like a charging bull. Olé! But whatever evolution gave Carnotaurus in the horns, it took away from in the arms department. This dino's teeny-weeny forelimbs were pretty much useless for hunting, defending itself . . . and let's not even talk about brushing its teeth.

↑ This dino's arms were even shorter than T. rex's!

All bite. ↗
No bark.

78 | Cretaceous Period

Kosmoceratops.
(Ornate horned face)

- 83–70 MYA
- Herbivore
- 15 ft. (4.5 m)

A worthy contender for the Fanciest Prehistoric Face Award, Kosmoceratops takes ornamentation to a whole new level! It had a dazzling display of frills, flaps, and horns adorning its noggin. This Cretaceous herbivore may not be as famous as its cousin, Triceratops, but it certainly was a whole lot fancier.

A fringe with benefits.

Looks like somebody found the blueberry patch.

Euoplocephalus.
(Well-armored head)

- 83–66 MYA
- Herbivore
- 16 ft. (5 m)

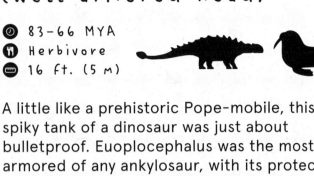

A little like a prehistoric Pope-mobile, this spiky tank of a dinosaur was just about bulletproof. Euoplocephalus was the most heavily armored of any ankylosaur, with its protective plates even extending over its face (hence its name). But if that wasn't enough to defend itself, it could whip its strong, club-like tail to fend off hungry, less vegetarian dinosaurs.

Feel like a club sandwich?

Spiky vegetarian.

Euoplocephalus: so defensive.

Reinforced rump.

80 | Cretaceous Period

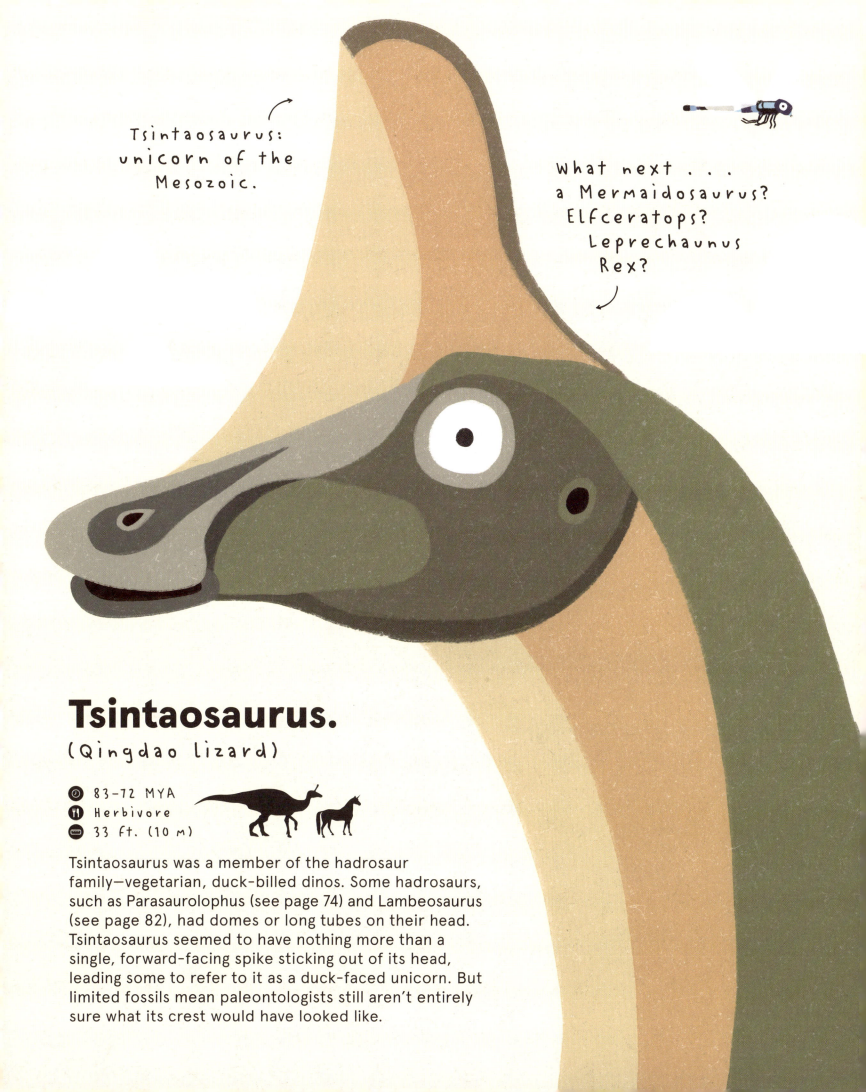

Tsintaosaurus: unicorn of the Mesozoic.

What next... a Mermaidosaurus? Elfceratops? Leprechaunus Rex?

Tsintaosaurus.
(Qingdao lizard)

- 83–72 MYA
- Herbivore
- 33 ft. (10 m)

Tsintaosaurus was a member of the hadrosaur family—vegetarian, duck-billed dinos. Some hadrosaurs, such as Parasaurolophus (see page 74) and Lambeosaurus (see page 82), had domes or long tubes on their head. Tsintaosaurus seemed to have nothing more than a single, forward-facing spike sticking out of its head, leading some to refer to it as a duck-faced unicorn. But limited fossils mean paleontologists still aren't entirely sure what its crest would have looked like.

Lambeosaurus.
(Lambe's lizard)

- 83–70 MYA
- Herbivore
- 49 ft. (15 m)

Turns out that Cretaceous critters loved their showy headgear! With its impressive bony crest, the duck-billed Lambeosaurus was no exception to the trend. Because its nostrils extended up into the crest, it is thought that it may have been used to improve their sense of smell or to make loud sounds, similar to Parasaurolophus (see page 74).

↑ Flock jokes? Herd 'em all.

Super-snout.

Look out for king-sized boogers. Eew.

What came after the chirostenotes? Its tail.

Rhinorex.
(Nose king)

- 75 MYA
- Herbivore
- 30 ft. (9 m)

Whoever named the "nose king" clearly had a sense of humor, but that said, Rhinorex definitely got more than its fair share of schnoz. Part of the duck-billed dinosaur family that included Tsintaosaurus (see page 81) and Lambeosaurus (see page 82), it's believed they would produce loud blasts and blares from their majestic nose to communicate with other herd members.

84 | Cretaceous Period

▶ Halszkaraptor.
(Halszka's thief)

- 75–71 MYA
- Piscivore
- 18 in. (45 cm)

With its long, swan-like neck, small, mallard-shaped body, and bird-like bill, at first glance this dino looks more than a bit like something you might see in the park at the weekend. However, Halszkaraptor was not a direct ancestor of modern birds, but a member of the dromaeosaurs—a family of non-avian theropods, which included Velociraptor.

This swan's no swan.

▼ Chirostenotes.
(Narrow handed)

- 79–67 MYA
- Omnivore
- 6 ft. (1.7 m)

So, you know how cassowaries are some of the most dangerous birds in existence, largely because of the sharp claw on the back of their foot? Well, imagine one that had arms with three similarly sharp talons on each side and you'd have Chirostenotes . . . or more like Chirostenoooooooo!

Weaponized wings. Argh!

Terrifying turbo turkey.

Cretaceous Period | 85

Cretaceous can opener.

The gnarliest gnashers!

Masiakasaurus.
(Vicious lizard)

- 72–66 MYA
- Carnivore
- 7 ft. (2 m)

Look into any dinosaur's mouth and you'd most likely be screaming in fright, but this monster takes terrifying teeth to a whole new level. Those forward-facing frontal fangs might not have made for the best school photos, but they would have proved incredibly useful for snaring fish from the water's edge and catching other small, fast-moving prey.

Fibbosaurus.

Eats real boys for breakfast. No lie!

▲ Qianzhousaurus.
(Qianzhou lizard)

- 72–66 MYA
- Carnivore
- 21 ft. (6.3 m)

This medium-sized theropod lived alongside its rather more famous cousin, T. rex, but while T. rex was teased for its comedically short arms, Qianzhousaurus had a different problem. Known for having an exceptionally long snout, it is often nicknamed "Pinocchio rex."

▶ Therizinosaurus.
(Scythe lizard)

- 72–66 MYA
- Herbivore
- 33 ft. (10 m)

Picture an emu the size of an elephant, and then imagine it with arms that each carry a handful of sword-like claws 3 feet (1 meter) long! But fear not, this dino didn't use those colossal claws for catching its dinner (plants don't tend to require such swashbuckling cutlery). Instead, they were for helping it to avoid *being* dinner. Unable to outrun its predators, scientists think it would have instead stood its ground, swinging its gigantic claws to defend itself.

Therizinosaurus had the longest claws of any animal ever.

En garde!

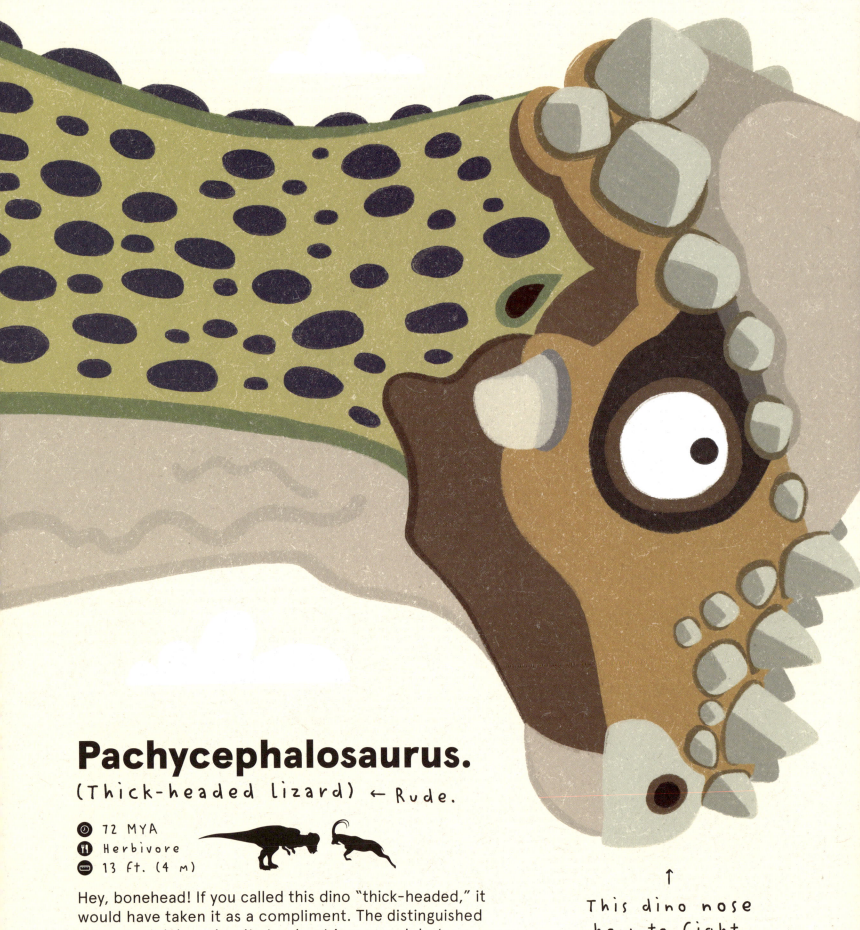

Pachycephalosaurus.
(Thick-headed lizard) ← Rude.

- 72 MYA
- Herbivore
- 13 ft. (4 m)

Hey, bonehead! If you called this dino "thick-headed," it would have taken it as a compliment. The distinguished dome certainly makes it stand out in a crowd, but scientists think that Pachycephalosaurus may have used its colossal cranium in head-butting contests.

↑ This dino nose how to fight.

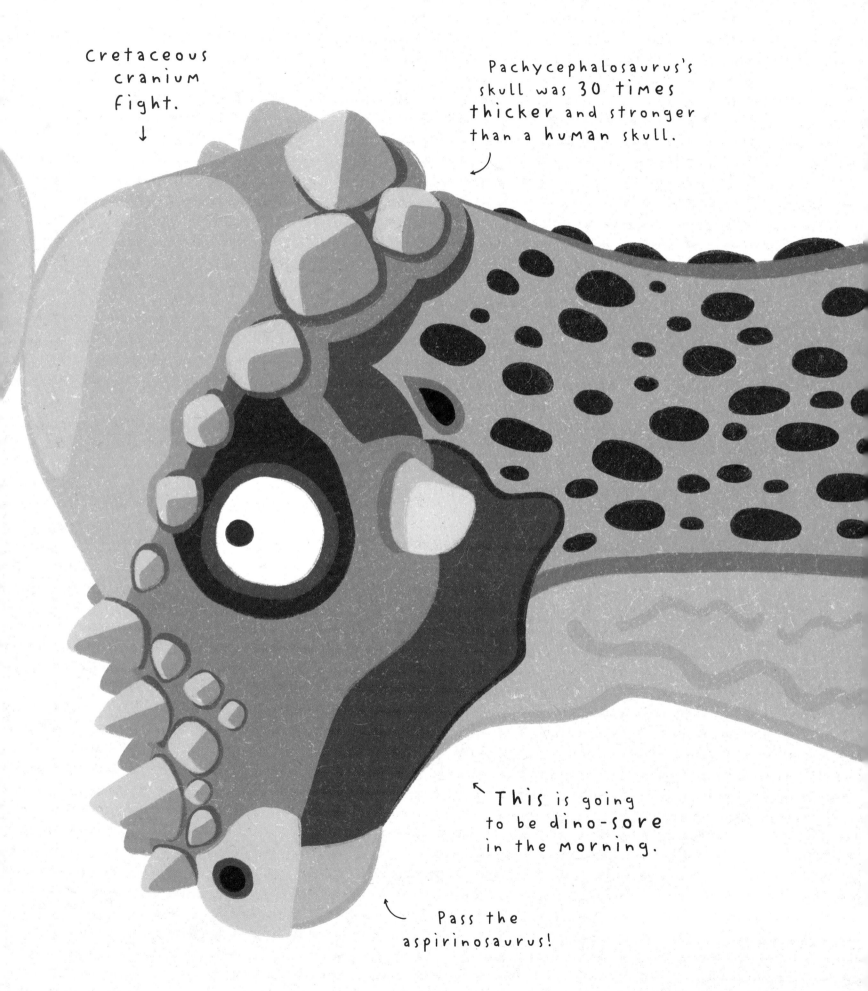

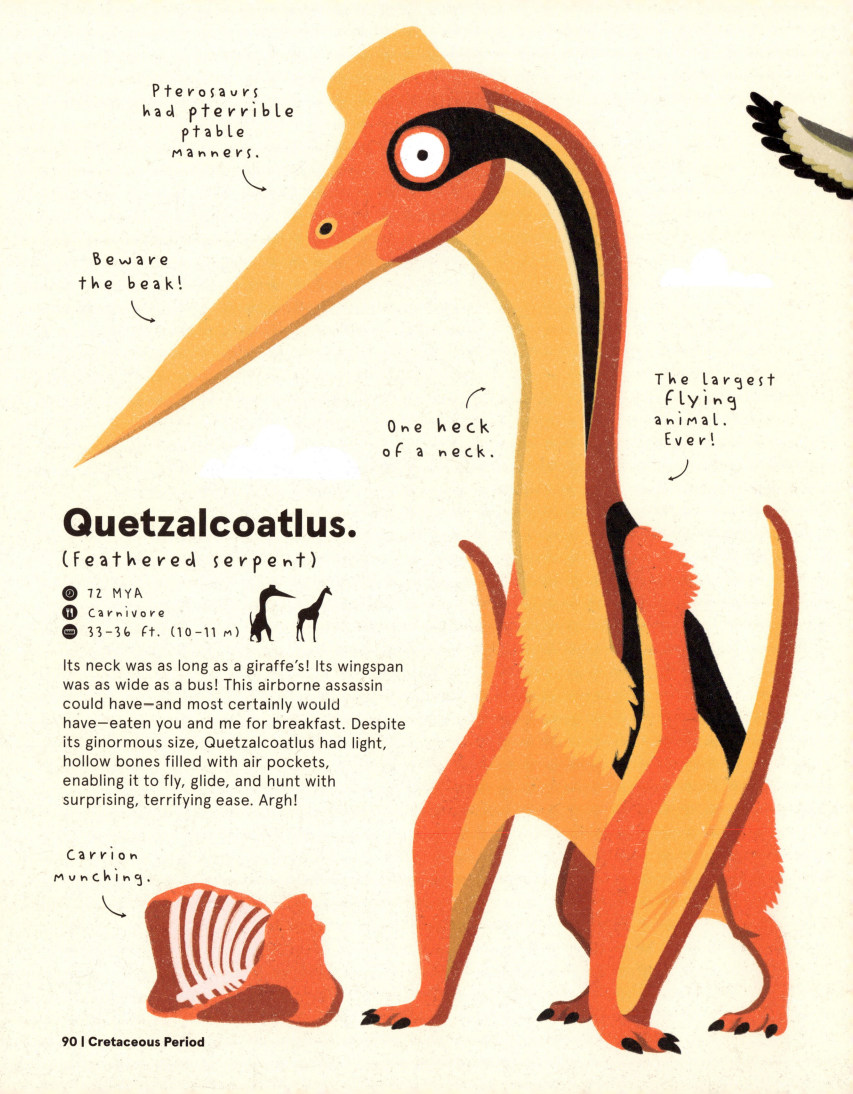

Pterosaurs had pterrible ptable manners.

Beware the beak!

One heck of a neck.

The largest flying animal. Ever!

Quetzalcoatlus.
(Feathered serpent)

- 72 MYA
- Carnivore
- 33–36 ft. (10–11 m)

Its neck was as long as a giraffe's! Its wingspan was as wide as a bus! This airborne assassin could have—and most certainly would have—eaten you and me for breakfast. Despite its ginormous size, Quetzalcoatlus had light, hollow bones filled with air pockets, enabling it to fly, glide, and hunt with surprising, terrifying ease. Argh!

Carrion munching.

What Mononykus lacked in hands, it made up for in speed. →

← The name checks out.

▲ Mononykus.
(One claw)

- 70 MYA
- Carnivore
- 3 ft. (1 m)

If you think poor old T. rex had embarrassingly small hands, spare a thought for Mononykus! In place of hands, it had a single 3-inch (7-centimeter) claw at the end of each arm. The claws don't look especially useful, but scientists think they may have evolved to open termite mounds or scratch insects from their nests, just like modern-day anteaters use their own claws.

▶ Nedoceratops.
(Insufficient horned face)

- 67 MYA
- Herbivore
- 23–30 ft. (7–9 m)

Everything we know about this species of ceratopsian comes from the discovery of a single fossilized skull. Some scientists say that Nedoceratops was a distinct species, while others think the skull belonged to a slightly weird—or at least, less spiky than usual—Triceratops.

This face looks sufficiently horned from here.

↑ Nedoceratops. Not pictured: Nedocerabottom.

Cretaceous Period | 91

The end?

About sixty-six million years ago, a city-sized asteroid 6–9 miles (10–15 kilometers) in diameter) crashed into the Earth, near present-day Mexico. As you might imagine, the impact of this asteroid was less than ideal for all involved. It caused sudden and devastating changes to the Earth's climate and ecosystems, leading to the extinction of over three-quarters of all species on the planet.

This extinction marked the end of the Cretaceous Period. But—despite what you may have heard—it did not wipe out *all* of the dinosaurs. One small set of weirdosauruses survived. Those plucky and adaptable two-legged feathered dinos we know as birds survived. That's right—penguins, parrots, falcons, and finches aren't merely the descendants of dinosaurs, they *are* dinosaurs.

Life on our home planet has changed a lot since the time of the dinosaurs. It's little wonder they come off as a bit weird! What do you think the inhabitants of Earth sixty-six million years in the future will make of the bones of elephants, platypuses, and aye-ayes? Or those kooky upright apes with giant brains? Let's not forget, the peculiar features that make these creatures seem so odd all evolved for

a reason. Every frill, quill, tooth, and claw evolved to help each animal survive and thrive in its particular environment. What we find weird is simply a matter of perspective. What's strange to you may appear perfectly normal to someone (or something) else. We all experience the world through our own very particular view of reality, and we're all delightfully weird, in our own peculiar way.

Index.

what comes after extinction? →
Y-stinction.

Amargasaurus 64–65
Ambopteryx 54
Anchiornis 48
ankylosaurs 40, 56, 80
Antarctica 42
Archaeopteryx 59
archosaurs 10
Arizonasaurus 20–21
Atopodentatus 19

Bajadasaurus 62
birds 48, 59, 63, 93
Brachiosaurus 55
burrowing dinosaurs 71

Caelestiventus 36
Carnotaurus 78
Carnufex 30
Caudipteryx 68
ceratopsians 58, 77, 79, 91
Chaoyangsaurus 58
Chilesaurus 57
Chirostenotes 85
claws 33, 69, 85, 87, 91
colors, dinosaur 48
Concavenator 63
cooling 21, 57, 65, 72
crests 42, 43, 47, 52, 81, 82
Cretaceous Period 60, 93
crocodiles 30, 36
Cryolophosaurus 42

Daemonosaurus chauliodus 37
Dicraeosaurus 50

Dilophosaurus 43
Drepanosaur 33

Einiosaurus 77
Eotitanosuchus 14
Epidexipteryx 48
Eretmorhipis 16
Erythrosuchus 18
Eudimorphodon 35
Euoplocephalus 80

96

extinction 12, 15, 92–93

feathers 44, 47, 48–49, 59, 63, 68
filter-feeders 17, 19, 31, 69
flying and gliding 27, 35, 36, 48–49, 66, 90
fossilized bones 4–6
Fruitadens 58

Gargoyleosaurus 56
Gigantoraptor 76–77
Guanlong 52

hadrosaurs 81, 82, 84
Halszkaraptor 85
heads, domed 34, 81, 88
Henodus 31
herds 74, 77, 83, 84
Hesperosaurus 56–57
hoaxes 16
horns 18, 77, 78
Huayangosaurus 45
Hupehsuchus 17
Hyperodapedon 24–25
Hypuronector 26–27

Incisivosaurus 67

Jeholopterus 49
Jurassic Period 38

Kosmoceratops 79
Kulindadromeus 44

Lambeosaurus 82–83
Lesothosaurus 40

Longisquama 28
Lufengosaurus 43
Lystrosaurus 15

Mamenchisaurus 53
Masiakasaurus 86
Mastodonsaurus 17
Mesozoic Era 11
Metoposaurus 29
Microraptor 66
Mononykus 91

necks 22, 53
Nedoceratops 91
Nigersaurus 66
noses 55, 84
nut-eaters 70
Nyctosaurus 75

Oryctodromeus 71
Owen, Sir Richard 9

Pachycephalosaurus 88–89
Parasaurolophus 74
Pegomastax 41
Placerias 29
platypuses 16
Proceratosaurus 47
Psittacosaurus 70
Pterodaustro 69
pterosaurs 24, 35, 36, 49, 53, 69, 75, 90

Qianzhousaurus 87
Quetzalcoatlus 90
quills 41, 58

recreating dinosaurs 6–9
reptiles 10
Rhamphorhynchus 53
Rhinorex 84

sails 21, 65, 72
sauropods 43, 44, 50
Scelidosaurus 40

Scleromochlus 24
Sharovipteryx 35
Shringasaurus 18
Shunosaurus 44
Silesaurus 32
sounds 74, 82, 84
spines and spikes 21, 45, 50, 54, 56, 62, 65, 72
Spinosaurus 72
Stagonolepis 30
stegosaurs 40, 45, 54, 56
Suzhousaurus 69
swimming 72

tails 27, 33, 44, 56, 68, 80
Tanystropheus 22
teeth 35, 37, 41, 58, 66–67, 86
Teraterpeton 32
Terrestrisuchus 36
Thalattosaurus 23
Therizinosaurus 87
theropods 42, 63, 67, 85, 87
Thrinaxodon 15
Tianchisaurus 46
tree-dwellers 27, 28, 33, 35, 54
Triassic Period 12
Triopticus primus 34
Tsintaosaurus 81

Yingshanosaurus 54

← what comes after y-stinction?
Z-end.